Louise Borden & Trish Marx

TOUCHING the SKY

The flying adventures of Wilbur and Orville Wright

illustrated by **Peter Fiore**

Margaret K. McElderry Books • New York   London   Toronto   Sydney   Singapore

introduction

All over the world,
people have heard of Wilbur and Orville Wright,
the two brothers from Dayton, Ohio,
who invented the world's first powered airplane.
The Wright Brothers!
It seems almost as if Wilbur and Orville
became *one* famous person.

Some of us already know bits and pieces
of Wilbur and Orville's amazing life story:

that their grandfather was a wagon maker,
that their mother, Susan, built a sled for the family,
that their father, Milton, was a minister
who encouraged his five children
to be curious about the world,
to be readers and writers and thinkers.

Some of us know that Wilbur and Orville
grew up as ordinary boys in a small Ohio town.
They made kites and flew them with their friends.
They were good students but they did not attend college.
They never married but they were close to their family.

They worked together on many things:
printing a newspaper,
riding and repairing bicycles,
and later building and selling them.

The Wright brothers were good record keepers.
They kept diaries and notebooks.
They took photographs and developed the plates themselves.
They wrote hundreds of letters during their lives.
And when they decided to build gliders
and later their famous planes—
or flyers as they were then known—
they began from scratch:
step by step by step.

Lots of testing and experiments.
Lots of thinking together and talking together.
They looked at problems in new ways,
then tried to find the right answers.
Wilbur and Orville worked as a team
in their workshop in Dayton,
and on the steamy, hot days
and the bitter cold days at Kitty Hawk, in North Carolina,
and in spite of those who said, "It can't be done!"

When the Wright brothers actually flew at Kitty Hawk
on December 17, 1903,
most of the world didn't stop and take notice.
But finally by 1909
the world had realized how special these brothers were.
Wilbur and Orville had become the first celebrities
of the twentieth century.
In September of that year
the Wright brothers made some remarkable flying exhibitions.
The stories that follow are about those historic flights in 1909.

Wilbur and the Red Canoe

In September of 1909
the city of New York gave itself a huge party.
It was the biggest party
in the city's three-hundred-year history
and it lasted for *two weeks*!

Everyone was invited to the celebration:
more than three million New Yorkers,
an international fleet of ships,
the barges and tugboats of New York's busy harbor,
people from other cities and states,
and one very, very special guest:

   the famous Mr. Wilbur Wright.

New York had a lot to be proud of.
It was the biggest city in the country,
and the second-biggest city in the world.
And it was probably the noisiest,
with its babble of languages,
because in 1909
most New Yorkers were immigrants,
and the city's streets were teeming with people:
Dutch . . . Italians . . . Greeks . . .
Jews . . . Poles . . . Russians . . .
Germans . . . Irish . . . Arabs . . .
Indians . . . Turks . . . Czechs . . .
French . . . Japanese . . .
Chinese . . . Portuguese . . . Lebanese. . . .
The new Americans living in New York City
came from many continents of the world.

New York City called its party
the Hudson-Fulton Celebration
so that New Yorkers could honor
two important men who were part
of the city's long, rich history:
Henry Hudson and Robert Fulton.

In September of 1609
the explorer Henry Hudson sailed into
the wide river that bears his name.
He rowed ashore from his ship, the *Half Moon*,
and stood on the tip of the island
we now call Manhattan.
Until then
canoes paddled by Delaware tribes
had glided back and forth
across the waters of this majestic river.

New Yorkers also wanted to celebrate Robert Fulton.
He, too,
was a famous navigator of the Hudson River.
In 1807
Fulton launched his wonderful steamboat,
the first in the world,
from the shore of Manhattan.
The *Clermont* churned noisily past the city on its way upriver to Albany.
Crowds of New Yorkers cheered and waved.
Speed and progress!

Always
New York was a city on the move,
a city of invention,
a city of change.

So of course,
New York's party
would be huge and grand!

Everyone took part in the two-week celebration.
Parades of soldiers and sailors!
Flags and bands!
Speeches! Festivals! Costumes! Dancing!
Three hundred years of history!
So much to celebrate!

Hundreds of thousands of children
marched in parades,
school by school,
neighborhood by neighborhood.
Plays! Songs!
A canoe-building day!
The celebration stretched from New York Harbor
past Central Park and on to Grant's Tomb.

And the nights were just as exciting.
On the East River,
crews of workmen hung long ropes of electric lights
on the historic Brooklyn Bridge
and other bridges to Manhattan.
Even more lights were hung along the outlines
of buildings and monuments,
such as the arch in Washington Square,
the fancy Plaza Hotel,
and the new Flatiron Building.

The fifty-seven warships of the international fleet
were festooned with light bulbs and lanterns.

Everyone in the city waited . . .
and waited
and waited.
Then a special signal was given.
At the same moment,
switches were turned on all over the city.
How exciting! How modern!

On September 18,
a week before the party began,
Wilbur Wright packed his suitcase
at his family's house on Hawthorne Street
in Dayton, Ohio,
put $180 in his wallet
for his travel expenses,
and took a train to New York City
with his mechanic, Charlie Taylor.

Wilbur Wright had agreed to give
a *public* exhibition of his flying skills.
Wilbur loved history.
He loved geography.
And he was a patriotic citizen.
Plus, he would earn some money for these flights.

This is why Wilbur said yes
when he and Orville were asked to be special guests
at New York's celebration.
Orville couldn't attend because
the Wrights had signed a contract
with a German company.
The brothers decided that Orville would fly in Germany
and Wilbur would attend New York's celebration.

Wilbur checked into the Park Avenue Hotel
and made sure that his flyer had arrived safely
in its boxes and crates.

The city of New York was ready
for its famous guest.
They had cleared a special field on Governors Island,
a small island in New York Harbor.
It was wide and flat:
the perfect place for Wilbur
to take off and land.
The city had also built a big wooden shed
with a pair of sliding doors
for Wilbur's flyer.
Most New Yorkers had never seen a flying machine—
on the ground or in the air.
This would be the very first time!
But everyone had heard of Wilbur and Orville Wright.

Wilbur had one week to get ready.
He and Charlie Taylor had important work to do!
They carefully assembled the flyer in its shed,
part by part:
wings and struts and spars and wires,
rudders and engine and levers and seat.
Day by day,
the silver-and-white machine
took its unique shape.

Wilbur and Charlie worked
with a few trusted workmen.
They still wanted to protect their process
until their patents were secure.

Wilbur was a brave but careful airman.
He knew his flyer was the best in the world,
but what if, for some reason, his engine failed
when he was flying over water?

Both of the Wright brothers
had already had their share of mishaps and crashes:
bumps and bruises,
torn wings and broken struts.
Flying in tricky wind currents could be difficult,
and Wilbur knew the tall buildings in New York City
would create sudden gusts.

Wilbur Wright loved to solve problems.
After all, like Orville,
he was a methodical scientist . . .
and, some said, a genius.
But Wilbur was a practical,
down-to-earth Dayton man as well.
He and Orville were used to finding
unusual but *simple* ways to solve problems,
first when they built bicycles,
later when they built kites and gliders,
and now when they kept improving
their flying machines.
So . . .
how to fly *safely* over New York's harbor?
Wilbur did his usual quiet thinking,
and then he talked to Charlie Taylor.

On the day before his first exhibition flight,
Wilbur walked out of his fine hotel
dressed in a plain, dark suit and tie,
a high, starched collar,
and a bowler hat.

He walked swiftly, with a purpose, down Park Avenue.
The buildings of New York
were much much taller than those in Dayton!
Then he walked down Broadway,
the busy street that back in Henry Hudson's days
had been a trading trail for the Delaware tribes.
He stopped at 814 Broadway,
the Folsom Arms Company,

a store that sold canoes and boats in Manhattan,
and went inside.
Wilbur Wright and his mechanic
had decided that the practical way
to fly safely over water
was to buy a canoe,
seal it with a watertight cover,
and suspend it from the skids of his flyer.
That way, if he crashed
and had to land on the water,
the canoe would help keep his flyer afloat.
Wilbur carefully chose a red "Indian Girl" Rushton canoe
and had it delivered to his shed on Governors Island.

While the city was getting ready
for its dozens of parades and events,
Wilbur stayed away from the crowds.
Only a few people were permitted
to visit the special shed.
Wilbur didn't have time to shake everybody's hand.
He needed to get his flyer ready.
He and Charlie worked from early in the morning
until late at night.

Now, at last,
Wilbur believed his machine was in A+ condition
and ready to go.
Underneath the silver-and-white flyer,
the red canoe with its canvas top
made a long slash of color.
Two American flags were attached to the front rudders,
and one on the rear of the machine.
The Hudson-Fulton Committee couldn't wait
for Wilbur to fly his machine.
Nor could the New York press.

With their pencils behind their ears,
the reporters asked Wilbur dozens of questions:
"Is your flyer ready?"
"How will the wind affect your flying?"
"How high will you fly? How fast?"
"Will you succeed in being the first to fly
over American waters?"
"Flying over those warships
will be dangerous. . . .
Are you afraid, Mr. Wright?"

Wilbur Wright stood in the shed on Governors Island and dusted off his hands
and answered the questions
in his calm, confident voice.

He knew that these days he and Orville
were front-page news across the country.
But Wilbur was no show-off.
And he didn't brag when he talked.
Even though he and his younger brother
were now famous throughout the world,
Wilbur was still his old Dayton, Ohio, self:
quiet, modest, and polite.
He had a strong faith
in the flying machines he built with Orville.
They had designed each part of their several flyers
with thought and care and hard work.

Wilbur knew that the flyer here in New York City would run just fine.

On September 25,
the day that New York's party officially began,
Wilbur and Charlie Taylor tested and tuned up the flyer.

The next day was Sunday.
Wilbur spent the whole day resting in his hotel room.
He and Orville had never flown on a Sunday.
They always respected their father Milton's belief
that the Sabbath was the day of rest.

For the past weeks in September,
Wilbur had been reading in the newspapers
about Orville and their sister, Katharine, in Germany.
Orville was making some terrific public flights
above the crowds in Berlin.
Soon it would be Wilbur's turn . . . in New York!

On Monday and Tuesday
the weather was rainy.
The skies were gray and full of high winds.
New Yorkers were waiting and waiting.
Everyone knew that as soon as the weather improved,
Wilbur Wright would attempt his flights.
Wilbur had promised the city
he would fly more than just once.

Finally on Wednesday, September 29,
the weather was perfect.
The wind was light and steady from the west.
Early that morning
Wilbur left the Park Avenue Hotel
and rode on the government ferry over to Governors Island.

There was a flurry of several hundred onlookers
who had been given special passes
to watch Wilbur's takeoff:
dignitaries and important New Yorkers,
soldiers in their khaki uniforms,
newspaper reporters and workmen.

An extra-long track had been laid across the sandy field.
This wooden rail was another Wright invention
to help launch the flyer.

The Wright flyer had no wheels.
It would take off into the air from the rail
and then land on the smooth skids
that looked like big skis under the lower wing.

Soldiers and workmen pushed and pulled the flyer
out of the shed and slid it onto the track.

The flags on Wilbur's flying machine fluttered in the breeze.
Workmen began to spin the two smooth spruce propellers.
The silver paint gleamed in the sun.
Fast . . . then faster . . . the propellers sliced the air.
The engine started up
with a loud rattle and pop.
The propellers spun round and round,
faster . . . faster . . .
until they were just a blur of pale gray.
Wilbur calmly climbed onto his seat.
Beside him was a life preserver,
strapped to the flyer.
It was 8:57 A.M.
Wilbur Wright buttoned his coat,
pulled down his cap,
and *then he was off!*

Up, up, up!

The flyer rose in the air to the cheers of the onlookers.

Then it turned,
crossing over the choppy Buttermilk Channel,
and circled back to Governors Island.
Astonishing!
The flyer swooped over some tugboats.
Then over a few more.
Whirring . . . turning.
Toot! Too-oot! Too-oot!
The boats saluted Wilbur with their horns and whistles
in the best harbor style.

Wilbur's first flight on that September day
lasted seven minutes and ten seconds.
He had traveled for two miles.
Wilbur landed the flyer back on the field
with a thump and a spray of sand.
"That's the worst landing I've made in a long time . . . ,"
Wilbur later said.
But nobody cared.
They thought Wilbur Wright's flying skills were terrific.

Wilbur and Charlie Taylor
checked the parts of the flyer,
and then an hour later
Wilbur took off again.
This time his flight was even more spectacular.
By now the news of his earlier feat had quickly spread
throughout the harbor.

New Yorkers were ready for this second flight.
On the docks and piers
and in lower Manhattan,
they waited for a glimpse of Wilbur Wright's fabulous flyer.

The wind had switched to the southwest.
Wilbur took off into the light breeze.
He rose again . . .

Up, *up,* *up!*

This time,
Wilbur showed even more of his skill.
The flyer flashed in the sun
and rose high above the gulls in the harbor.
It soared and turned gracefully,
then headed to the Statue of Liberty!
Boats below slowed down.
Thousands of people looked up at the sky.

Wilbur Wright then circled the Statue of Liberty,
waist high.

At the same time,
the *Lusitania*,
the largest and grandest ocean liner in the world,
was passing through the harbor
on its way to Europe.
On her decks were crowds of passengers,
cheering,
yelling,
waving their hats.
The deep tones of the *Lusitania*'s horns and whistles
echoed across the water.
Wilbur could look down at the array of ships below.
He could look across to the statue he had just circled,
and to the tall smokestacks of the famous ocean liner.

This spectacular flight
included an impressive figure eight.
It lasted less than five minutes.
Wilbur had shown New York
how easily he could turn and circle,
how easily he could steer.
Wilbur Wright had perfect control and balance.
He knew the *feel* of flying,
of warping the wings,
twisting them in opposite directions by pulling on wires,
of adjusting the rudders,
of leaning into the turns,
of knowing the right speed.

Wilbur landed his machine as softly as a dove
and modestly said:
"The wind was at my back.
I was probably going at the rate
of a little over fifty miles an hour."
The committee then announced that Wilbur
would fly again later in the day.
They took their guest back to Manhattan on the ferry,
and at noon Wilbur was taken to the Singer Building
so he could view the city
and plan a route for an even bigger flight.

The imposing new Singer Building
stood at 149 Broadway, south of the store
in which Wilbur had purchased his red canoe.
It was New York's very first skyscraper,
then the tallest building in the world.
Wilbur took a ride in an elevator,
new and modern,
to the observation deck at the very top.

From there,
with a powerful telescope,
Wilbur had a bird's-eye view of everything:
To the south was the Statue of Liberty
and Governors Island.
To the west of the Singer Building
was the blue gray Hudson River,
full of sturdy piers and the warships
of the international fleet.
On the far shore of the Hudson was New Jersey.
Crowds of spectators
lined that shore of the river as well.

Wilbur turned his telescope
and looked the opposite way,
to the East River.
It was full of more piers and shipping
and the bustling Fulton Fish Market.
And there were the bridges
that brought thousands of workers
into the city of New York.
The harbor,
the busiest in the world,
was alive with ships and tugboats
of all shapes and sizes.

Down below
Wilbur saw streets clogged with horses and buggies,
some automobiles, streetcars, and handcarts.
He scanned the rooftops of the many tenements
with laundry lines
and hundreds of wooden water towers.

Now Wilbur was ready:
He had seen the Hudson
and checked the winds and the shoreline.
Soon he would attempt an even more exciting flight for the city of New York.

But by the time Wilbur returned to
Governors Island,
the winds over the harbor had picked up.
He made one twelve-minute flight,
circling the island.
New York would have to wait a little longer
to see his most daring flight.

For the next four days,
while the events of the celebration continued,
Wilbur's spectacular flight around the Statue of Liberty
was front-page news across the country.
Everyone in New York
waited for the return of good weather.
Then, on the morning of October 4,
an even larger crowd gathered at Governors Island,
almost two thousand people!
Wilbur didn't like the commotion
and said so.
But somehow all those people had managed
to get special passes to see Wilbur's shed
and his flyer's takeoff.

Once again
Wilbur took his seat on the wing of his flying machine.
And on this day,
as on every other day,
Wilbur Wright was a man with a clear and steady purpose.

Today he would give New York
his best public flight ever.

Then he was off the starting rail . . .

> *up . . . up . . . up . . . !*

The long red canoe was easy to spot in the sky
under the silver-and-white aeroplane.
The three U.S. flags fluttered smartly.
Those red, white, and blue colors
were a reminder to New Yorkers
of the greatness of America . . .
of the new home millions had found on her shores
and of the inventions and energy of her citizens.

Everywhere in New York,
people were ready.
They stood at the windows of hotels and offices.
They crowded the decks of the international fleet.
They hurried to the docks and the piers
along the harbor and the Hudson.
They pushed and shoved along the busy streets,
wanting to get a good view.
Wilbur Wright!
Flying above New York City!
The Hudson-Fulton Committee had made a plan
to let the city know about Wilbur's flight.
All over New York,
on ships and on bridges
and on the taller buildings,
colorful signal flags would alert the public
that Wilbur's flying machine was in the air.

This was the route of the flight:
from the sandy field on Governors Island,
across the New York harbor, and up the Hudson River.
The whistles and horns of thousands of boats filled the air.
People cheered
and pointed
and threw their hats in the air.
Wilbur's flyer soared and turned,
then headed north above the Hudson,
above the same river
that early tribes had paddled on in their canoes,
that Henry Hudson had sailed in his *Half Moon,*
that Fulton had steamed on in his *Clermont*.

Babies . . . children . . . parents . . . grandparents.
A million of the peoples of the world,
new Americans,
New Yorkers,
were watching.
In dozens of different languages,
people marveled at what they saw.

Wilbur flew above the water . . .
        past Battery Park and the Customs House . . .
        past the Chelsea Piers . . .
        past the Astor Hotel Roof Garden . . .
        past tall buildings and famous churches . . .
        past libraries. . . .

The cheers of the crowds were deafening.
Everywhere people looked up at the sky.
They held binoculars.
They stood on park benches and on walls.
They waved handkerchiefs! Caps! Hats! Parasols!

Wilbur could feel the currents of wind
swooshing through the buildings
and gusting toward the Hudson.
He held the flyer steady,
with practice and control.
Wilbur was proud of that flying machine,
and proud of the years of work with Orville.
Together
they had unlocked the secret of flight.
He knew their vision had changed the world
in a marvelous way.

Below Wilbur were hundreds of ships,
scattered along the river,
docked in their berths at the New York piers.
The ships were strung with lines and lines of fluttering flags.
Thousands and thousands of people lined the shore.

Wilbur and his wonderful flyer swept north up the Hudson.

One mile . . . then two miles . . .
then another . . .
then another . . .

Wilbur Wright knew exactly how and where to fly.
He was confident and he was calm.
Pinned on his suit was a tiny Hudson-Fulton ribbon.
Like those who had come before him,
Wilbur was making history.

Along the route
each new crowd of onlookers was astonished.

Remarkable! A flying machine!

See the flags on the rudders!

Is that a canoe?

And just one man!

Wilbur Wright!

Such a genius!

Truly,
a man of the future!

For many immigrant New Yorkers
the scene was merely *another* marvel
of this new city
and of this new country.
Seven miles . . . eight miles . . . nine miles . . .

On and on Wilbur flew,
faster than a horse and buggy,
faster than a tugboat or a ship,
faster than an automobile.
Flying!

In the distance to the north
was the large dome of Grant's Tomb.
It was a city landmark,
the burial place of President Ulysses S. Grant,
built as a symbol of national peace.
Grant, like Wilbur and Orville,
had grown up in Ohio.

Closer . . . closer . . .
And then,
ten miles from his takeoff
at Governors Island,
Wilbur reached Grant's Tomb
and made a graceful turn . . .
turning . . .
as he swept down
over the tall stacks and rigging
of the mighty British warship the *Drake*.

The noise of the spectators was tremendous.
The din of the ships' whistles was deafening.
New Yorkers and people in the boats on the river
knew that this was history
and that they, too, were a part of it.

Wilbur headed back down the Hudson
toward Governors Island.
The return trip, with the wind behind him,
was even faster.

Another mile . . . then another . . . then another . . .

twelve . . . fifteen . . . nineteen . . .

Twenty miles in thirty-three minutes and thirty-three seconds!
Up the Hudson River to Grant's Tomb and back!

Wilbur looked down at the Hudson River,
at the harbor full of ships.
He looked at the buildings of the biggest city in the country.
He heard the cheers and salutes
and the joy of a million New Yorkers.
Indeed,
it was the grandest sight Wilbur had ever seen.
He could hardly wait to tell Orville all about it.

"HIGHER, ORVILLE, HIGHER!"

By September of 1909
everyone in Europe
had heard about Wilbur and Orville Wright
and their amazing flights in a flying machine.

But until 1908, just one year before,
not many people had seen them fly.

Orville and Wilbur were very private people
with great respect for their father's wishes.
Their father, Milton, believed the family
was the most important thing—
and that family members were the people you could most trust.
So Orville and Wilbur didn't show their great secret of flying
to the world until they were sure
it was the right time to do so.
European aviators had been trying to fly for years.
They watched birds of different shapes and sizes fly,
and thought there must be many different ways
that man could fly too.

But the Wright brothers knew there was only one way
to fly like a bird:
by soaring
and by *turning, turning, turning*.
The turning was as important as the soaring,
and no one could turn their flying machines the way
Orville and Wilbur could their Wright flyer.

In 1908
Wilbur and Orville were ready to show their flyer,
and how it could turn,
to small groups of people in America and in Europe,
people they had hoped would want to buy flying machines from them.

Orville stayed in America
to do test flights for government officials
while Wilbur sailed to France,
taking with him his flyer, in many parts, in crates.

When Wilbur unpacked the wood, the wire, and the cloth—
the pieces of his flying machine—
and carefully put them together,
the French laughed.

They called him *le bluffeur*, the bluffer,
and they called his flyer a *phantom machine*.

But on Saturday, August 8, at Le Mans,
the evening broke clear and windless.
The weather was the finest for flying in weeks.
Wilbur readied his flyer
and rose in the air,
and the world of flying changed forever.

Wilbur soared like an eagle.
He turned like an eagle,
making two rounds over the field.
In two minutes he landed,
satisfied he had shown what his flyer could do.

The Frenchmen watching below were stunned.
Even Bleriot, a famous French aviator
who had his own flyer, was stunned.
Wilbur could *turn* his flying machine
as they had only dreamed of doing.
He could *soar* while they could only *hop*.

Instead of *bluffeurs*,
the Wright brothers became *Les Premiers Hommes-oiseaux*—
the most important flying men.
Even Wilbur's hat became famous.
The French raced to buy a new "Veelbur Reet"
just like the soft cloth cap
Wilbur had borrowed from Orville
for his trip to Europe.

News of Wilbur's flights at Le Mans swept through France.
Crowds of military officers and aviators,
a few kings and queens, farmers,
and children of every age
"came to see the 'great white bird' make figure eights in the air."
Wilbur wrote to Orville that
"princes and millionaires seemed as thick as fleas."

After Wilbur's flights in France,
people were crazy about this new thing—this *flying*.
They had seen photographs in the newspapers;
they had read about the fancy medals and honors
heaped upon the brothers.
The world now recognized the *importance* of Wilbur and Orville's ideas
and experiments
and quiet, hard work
in their bicycle shop in Dayton
and on the windblown sand beaches at Kitty Hawk.

In September of 1909
it was Orville's turn to travel to Europe,
to show the world—the public—
the latest in loops and figure eights,
and takeoffs and landings.
Orville was also a businessman.
He had to show the people who wanted to form a company
how to make and sell the flyer
and what it could do.
And Orville had to train pilots for the new flyers.

Orville and his sister, Katharine, sailed for London,
then traveled to Berlin,
the busy capital of Germany.
The Europeans loved Katharine,
her warm smile,
her stylish clothes,
and the way she took care of her brothers.
She charmed their kings and queens
with her manners and her dignity.
By the time she took this trip
with Orville to Germany,
she was known as "the famous woman from America."

The Germans had seen *dirigibles,*
large, long, balloon-like flying machines
that moved slowly
and turned slowly.

But they had waited a long time to see an aeroplane.

When Orville arrived at Tempelhof Field, outside Berlin,
where, centuries before, monks had lived and worked,
he saw crowds of people
who had come by foot,
by bicycle,
by motor car,
by dirigible,
by horse and buggy,
by hay wagon
to see this wonderful thing.

Thousands of men and women and children,
all ages of children,
had come to see a *flight*.
Two hundred thousand people had come.

Two hundred thousand German voices cheered wildly and loudly
for the famous younger Wright brother
in his dark gray three-piece suit and tie,
in his high starched collar,
and with his moustache waxed to neat points.

Orville walked out of the large shed built for the aeroplane,
through the wooden fence built to hold back the crowd,
and toward his flyer.
He looked up at the two flags fluttering in the breeze,
one for Germany and one for America.

"There he is!"
      "There's Orville Wright!"

The German kaiser and his empress,
the prince and princesses,
and foreign ambassadors had come to see him too.
Kaiser Friedrich Wilhelm of Germany was especially excited.
He had studied flying.
He knew what it had taken to make this machine.
He wanted his family—
his wife, Empress Viktoria Luise,
and his children,
especially the crown prince, Friedrich Wilhelm—
to see this historic event.

Knowing they were going to see something special,
the crowd cheered as the flyer was pulled from the shed
by eight strong men.
Katharine, in her stylish, new hat,
stood by the royal family and cheered too.

After one last check of the flyer,
Orville climbed onto the lower wing.
He sat upright in the center.
His legs hung over the front edge of the wing,
his back straight against the simple seat,
his hands on the levers that would raise or lower the rudders
and warp the wings, twisting them in opposite directions
so he could turn and soar and circle
high above Tempelhof Field.

He started the engine.
He dropped his hand,
a sign for the aeroplane to be sent down the wooden rail
that was part of the launching gear,
invented by Orville and Wilbur to give their flyers the speed
they needed to rise into the air.
The flyer sped along the rail,
skimmed the ground . . .
and . . .

Orville was in the air!

The crowd let out a whoop of disbelief
and blinked their eyes
and shook their heads.

Amazing . . . it was simply *amazing*!

Such a grand sight, and right here
at ancient Tempelhof Field,
outside their own city.

Orville stayed close to the earth at first,
turning and climbing slowly as he picked up speed.
The twenty-five horsepower engine
made loud staccato popping noises.
The propellers flashed in the sun.
Orville watched the wind rip at the strong muslin on the wings.
A few years earlier in Dayton
he had drawn the first pattern himself
and cut the cloth.
Wilbur had sewn the first wing coverings together
and later shown the workmen how to do it.

Orville listened to the engine.
An old friend and mechanic, Charlie Taylor,
had made the engine for their first flyer
after engine factories said it was impossible.
The Wright brothers were used to starting their ideas from scratch.
Orville knew just by listening if everything was working all right.
Now everything sounded fine.

Orville curved and looped,
high and low,
twenty-four miles in thirty-six minutes.
He sailed surely and gracefully
as photographers below snapped pictures.

When Orville landed,
people raced to meet him.
He had to leave Katharine and the kaiser's family
so they would not be crushed
by the jubilant crowd.

The crown prince, a young man in his twenties,
wanted more than anything to fly with Orville.
But how could Orville take up the future kaiser of Germany?
Many men had been killed testing flyers and trying to fly.
Orville knew he and Wilbur had the best machine in the world.
He knew he was the best pilot, with the most control.
But what about a gust of wind?
What about a wing spar that might break?
What about a wire that might snap?

Every day
Orville kept saying, "No, not today," to the crown prince,
until October 2 when he finally said,
"Yes, you may be my passenger today."
He had moved his flyer to Bornstedt Field, also close to Berlin.
As usual, thousands of people were crowding the field.
Horses and buggies lined the road,
next to bicycles and automobiles,
and people were walking there on foot,
hoping not to miss this grand sight.

The crown prince put on a coat
to save his fancy uniform from oil spatters.
Orville and the crown prince climbed onto the wing.
The crowd was stunned.

What was this?
The *crown prince* was going to fly?
Their prince Friedrich,
the future king of Germany,
was going on the flyer with Orville?

Together, with one German voice,
the crowd gave a mighty cheer.

"FLY HIGH, CROWN PRINCE!"

Once more, Orville started the engine.
Once more, Orville gave the signal.
And once more, the flyer skimmed the ground and lifted into the air.

Even though the crown prince was a brave sportsman,
Orville did not dare go higher than twenty-five feet.

"Higher, Orville, higher!"
Orville heard the crown prince's voice over the roar of the engine.
"Higher, Orville, higher!"

Orville climbed to seventy feet.
The trees looked like twigs.
The people looked like a great black ring surrounding the field.
For seven minutes Orville and the crown prince,
the first member of a royal family to fly in an aeroplane,
soared and circled over the crowds.

What an adventure!
"Crown Prince Wilhelm was my happiest passenger,"
Orville later said.
When they landed,
the band played, and three mighty cheers went up from the crowd
as they waved hats and handkerchiefs and parasols.
What could the crown prince do to show Orville how wonderful he felt?
He took off a jeweled pin he was wearing.
It had a crown set in rubies and the initial *W* set in diamonds.
The royal jewels sparkled in the sun.
As he pinned it on Orville's coat he said the *W* could as easily
stand for *Wright* as for *Wilhelm.*

Orville set many records in Germany.
He made the first night flight
from Bornstedt Field.
When he was ready to land,
the people watching had to turn the lights of their motorcars on
so he could see the field.

He had flown the longest flight ever with a passenger,
for one hour, thirty-five minutes, forty-six seconds.

He had flown the highest ever,
on September 9, reaching nine hundred two feet.

He had flown with a prince.

But he still wanted to prove more
to the Germans and the world.
He thought of Wilbur
at the grand festival in New York City,
hoping to fly over American waters for the first time.

What else could he do that day that would be daring and new?

"Higher, Orville, higher!" rang in his ears.

He looked up at the sky.
It was a fine day for flying.
The flyer was in perfect shape.
The crowd was waiting—
waiting, as one newspaper said,
for the poetry of flying.

Orville was the impulsive brother,
the one who loved making practical jokes,
the doer more than the thinker,
and he had a real touch for flying.

Orville motioned for his flyer to be put into position.
A small balloon had been let up at the end of a rope.
It went up five hundred twenty-five feet.

Orville knew that he could fly higher than that small balloon.
He knew he could fly higher than anyone had gone before.

Once more, Orville climbed onto the lower wing.
Once more, he gave the signal for the plane to race along the rail.
Once more that day, he rose into the air.

Orville circled around the field several times.
Then he flew far toward the east,
as if he were going to go to China.
But he gracefully curved around,
back down the field,
going up,
          up,
                higher in the air,

              all the way,

                    300 feet

                         400 feet

                              525 feet

until he sailed over the balloon.

But that was not enough,
not for Orville, not on this day.

He wanted to go higher.

He circled again
and again.
With each circle, he rose higher into the air.

700 feet

    800 feet

        1000 feet

Orville rose so high that the balloon was just a speck
moving in the winds.
He could see a long road stretching for miles.
He could see houses in a village, far away.
He could feel the crowd,
afraid, cheering, exhilarated,
somewhere down below.
He knew the crown prince was there too,
cheering with the crowd.

If he could only get high enough,
he would be all by himself
up there in the blue sky,
almost to the clouds.
He circled again,
a wide, clean circle up there in the blue.
And again,
and again.

1,100 feet

    1,200 feet

        1,400 feet

After fifteen minutes of steady climbing,
he knew he was higher than anyone had ever gone before.

Past 1,500 feet . . .

People on a steamer on a lake,
three miles away,
saw Orville soaring and turning in the sky.
"We thought it was a kite," they said.

Orville had flown to almost sixteen hundred feet!
This was nearly twice the record he had set only days before.

"The descent I made in five minutes," Orville said.
"I came down at a simply terrifying speed.
The whole machine shook, as it rushed through the air . . .
but the air was no colder,
or the wind resistance no greater . . .
than as in lower altitudes."

Those were Orville's words.

The crowd went wild!
A thousand hands reached out to touch the flyer.
In the confusion
a young boy ran under the fence,
onto the field.
He stared up, up, with large blue eyes
at the flyer coming down so fast.

A soldier on a swift horse raced to stop him,
afraid for the boy,
afraid for Orville.
The boy looked up at the panting horse.
He looked at the soldier, with his stern face.
Then he looked up again.
He could see only the flyer.
The soldier swooped up the boy
and carried him safely to his father,
a workman at the starting rail.

A few weeks later
Orville and Katharine left for home,
more famous than before.
Orville had proven the Wright flyer was the best in the world.
It could fly long distances with a passenger.
It could turn like an eagle.
It could fly higher than any aeroplane had ever flown.
It was safe enough for a prince.

He could hardly wait to return home
and tell Wilbur about his flying adventures.

epilogue

Wilbur, Orville, and Katharine returned to Dayton in the late fall of 1909.
They were famous and they were rich,
but they had not changed.
Other than Katharine's choice not to return to her teaching job
but to stay at home to help and support her brothers,
things went along pretty much the same for the Wright brothers.

They built a factory to make their new airplanes.
They taught the factory workers how to build the planes.
They experimented and tested new designs.
They perfected old designs.

They rose early and worked late.
They still argued far into the night
about this angle or that idea,
often changing each other's mind in the process
so that by morning, each found himself on the other side.

Wilbur was the one who tackled the business end,
going to the courts,
talking with lawyers and government officials,
trying to keep others from taking credit for his and Orville's ideas.

Only once did he and Orville fly together.
In 1910
they went up in one of their flyers.
Sitting side by side,
they flew a few circles
and landed safely.

That same day, with Wilbur watching from the ground,
Orville took up their father, Milton.
Orville loved to tell the story.
"He [Milton] kept saying, 'Higher, Orville, higher!'"

On one trip to Boston,
Wilbur fell ill with typhoid fever, a serious illness.
He returned home but kept working, even with a fever.
Finally he took to his bed,
wrote his will,
and died shortly after, in May of 1912.
Twenty-five thousand people viewed his casket,
and for three full minutes
the citizens of Dayton stopped everything they were doing
as they mourned an American hero.

Orville had lost his brother, his best friend,
his other half who knew the secrets of flying.
He was devastated,
but he carried on, built a large new home for his father
and sister and himself.
He saved the canoe Wilbur had carried under the flyer
on the historic New York City flights,
in honor and memory of Wilbur.
Today the canoe is on exhibit at
Carillon Historical Park in Dayton, Ohio,
with other Wright brothers memorabilia.

The Hudson-Fulton medal given to Wilbur
can be seen at the library of Wright State University in Dayton,
as can the tiny flag he wore during the flight.
The ruby and diamond pin given to Orville by the German crown prince
is still worn by a member of the Wright family.

Orville took over the business end.
He also kept inventing—toys, a toaster that would not burn the bread,
a special plumbing system for the new house.
And he still played practical jokes on his nieces and nephews
and laughed louder than any of them when they fell for his tricks.

Orville died in 1948.
The country mourned again, as they had for Wilbur.
Schools and city offices were closed early,
and fighter planes from nearby Wright Field flew in formation
over the funeral procession.

Planes were everywhere by then.
They had flown in both World War I and World War II.
They could fly high above earth.
They could travel at speeds of more than three hundred miles per hour.
Hundreds of ordinary people had flown on one.

There was even talk of traveling into space!

As a reporter had said so many years ago
when Wilbur flew over France,
"If Man could do this,
was there anything Man could not do?"

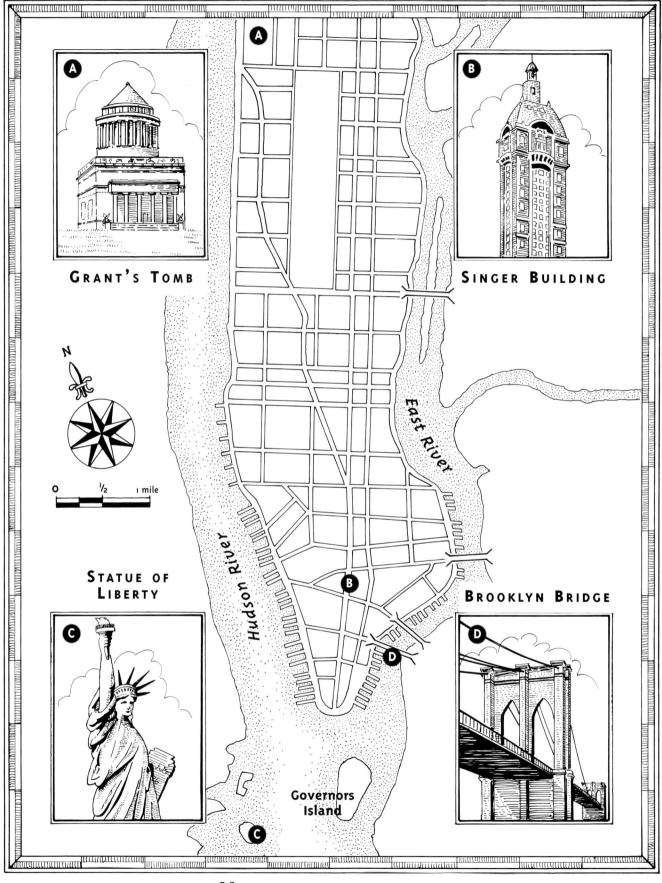

A GRANT'S TOMB

B SINGER BUILDING

N

0   ½   1 mile

STATUE OF
LIBERTY

Hudson River

East River

B

BROOKLYN BRIDGE

C

D

Governors
Island

D

MANHATTAN 1909

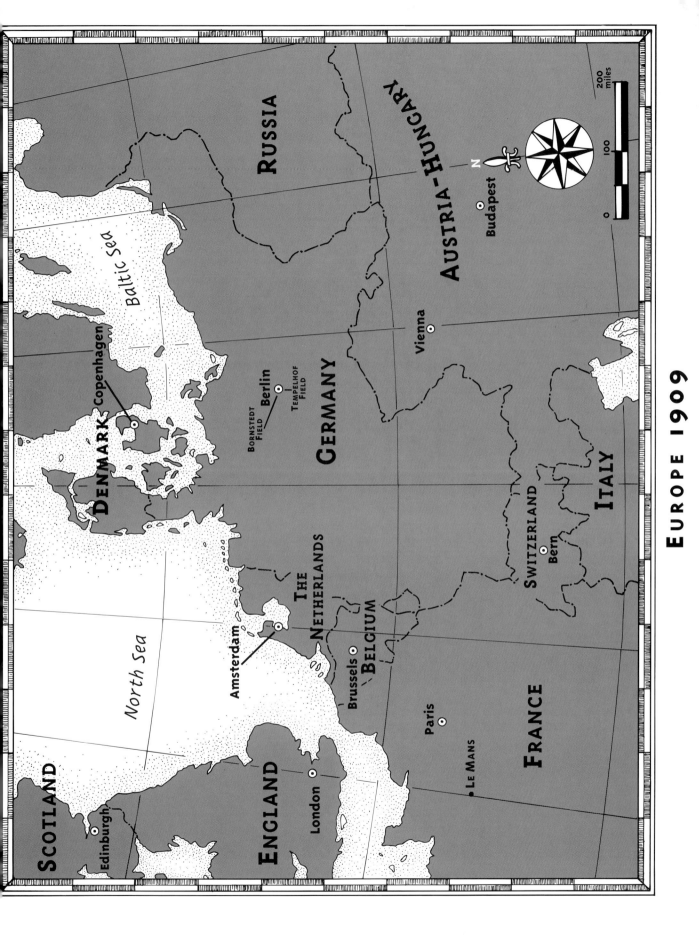

EUROPE 1909

AVIATION TIME LINE

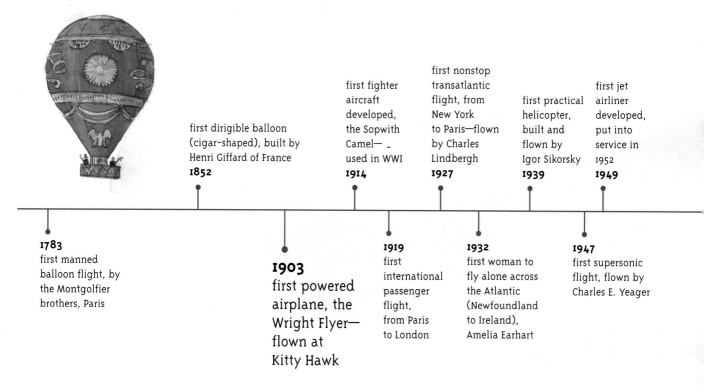

first fighter
aircraft
developed,
the Sopwith
Camel—
used in WWI
1914

first nonstop
transatlantic
flight, from
New York
to Paris—flown
by Charles
Lindbergh
1927

first practical
helicopter,
built and
flown by
Igor Sikorsky
1939

first jet
airliner
developed,
put into
service in
1952
1949

first dirigible balloon
(cigar-shaped), built by
Henri Giffard of France
1852

1783
first manned
balloon flight, by
the Montgolfier
brothers, Paris

1903
first powered
airplane, the
Wright Flyer—
flown at
Kitty Hawk

1919
first
international
passenger
flight,
from Paris
to London

1932
first woman to
fly alone across
the Atlantic
(Newfoundland
to Ireland),
Amelia Earhart

1947
first supersonic
flight, flown by
Charles E. Yeager

first transatlantic
jet airliner services,
between London
and New York
1958

first
Reconnaissance
aircraft, the
Blackbird
1964

first supersonic
airliner, the
Concorde
1967

first space
shuttle
launched, John
F. Kennedy Space
Center
1981

1957
first
unmanned
satellite
launched
into space,
the *Sputnik 1*
("Sputnik"
means "fellow
traveler"
in Russian)

1961
first American in
space, Alan B.
Shepard Jr.

1969
first moon
landing,
by Edwin E.
Aldrin Jr.,
who carried
a piece
of cloth
from the
Wright Flyer

1973
first space
station in
orbit, the
Skylab

2000
first launch of
Expedition One—the
International Space
Station (joint Russian,
American enterprise)

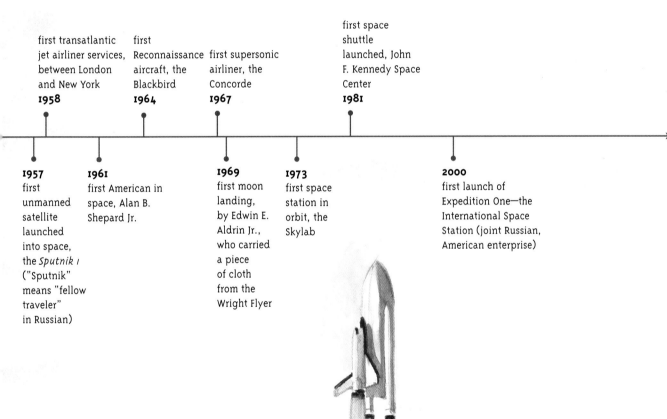

To Dad for keeping me grounded,
and Mom for teaching me to fly
—T. M.

For Catherine Ayars Borden
and also for Reeve
—L. B.

For Barbara, who makes almost all things possible
—P. F.

Acknowledgments

The authors would like to thank the Museum of the City of New York, the New York
Historical Society, the National Museum of the American Indian, the New York
Society Library, the Goethe Institute of New York, the Carillon Historical Park in
Dayton, Ohio, the Wilbur Wright Birthplace, John Hackenberg, Camilla Warrick, and
the Wright family.

And a special thank-you to John Sanford, Dawne Dewey, and Jane Wildermuth,
the Special Collections and Archives curators at the Wright State University Libraries.

Margaret K. McElderry Books • An imprint of Simon & Schuster Children's Publishing Division • 1230 Avenue of the Americas, New York, New York 10020 •
Text copyright © 2003 by Louise Borden and Trish Marx • Illustrations copyright © 2003 by Peter Fiore • All rights reserved, including the right of
reproduction in whole or in part in any form. • Book design by Ann Bobco and Sonia Chaghatzbanian • Map art by Rick Britton • The text for this book
is set in Triplex. • The illustrations for this book are rendered in watercolor. • Manufactured in China • 2 4 6 8 10 9 7 5 3 1 • Library of Congress
Cataloging-in-Publication Data • Borden, Louise. • Touching the sky : the flying adventures of Wilbur and Orville Wright /
Louise Borden & Trish Marx ; illustrated by Peter Fiore. • p. cm. • Summary: A look at how the Wright Brothers became the first celebrities of
the twentieth century through their 1909 public flying exhibitions in New York City and Germany. • ISBN 0-689-84876-5 (hardcover) •
1. Wright, Orville, 1871-1948—Journeys—New York—New York—Juvenile literature. 2. Wright, Wilbur, 1867-1912—Journeys—New York—New York—
Juvenile literature. 3. Wright, Orville, 1871-1948—Journeys—Europe—Juvenile literature. 4. Wright, Wilbur, 1867-1912—Journeys—Europe—Juvenile
literature. 5. Aeronautics—Flights—Juvenile literature. [1. Wright, Orville, 1871-1948. 2. Wright, Wilbur, 1867-1912. 3. Aeronautics—Flights.] I. Marx, Trish.
II. Fiore, Peter M., ill. III. Title. • TL540.W7 B67 2003 • 629.13'0092'273—dc21 • 2002012041

Wilbur Wright's quote on page 26 is from the *New York Evening Post* (29 September 1909).
His quote on page 30 is from the *New York Tribune* (30 September 1909).
His quote on page 44 is from a letter to Orville (9 August 1908).
Orville Wright's quote on page 56 is from the *New York World* (4 October 1909).

Glenn Curtiss, another American aviator and rival of the Wright brothers, was also asked to give a public exhibition at the Hudson-Fulton
Celebration. On September 29 he made a very brief test flight over Governors Island, and then left New York City.